Algrove Publishing Limited
36 Mill Street, P.O. Box 1238
Almonte, Ontario, Canada K0A 1A0

Telephone: (613) 256-0350
Fax: (613) 256-0360
Email: sales@algrove.com

Library and Archives Canada Cataloguing in Publication

Moore, Clement Clarke, 1779-1863
    The night before Christmas with puzzle pictures / [written by Clement Clarke Moore ; illustrated by Curtis Wager-Smith].

(Classic reprint series)
Reprint. First published: Philadelphia : Henry Altemus Co., 1907.
ISBN 1-897030-36-3

    1. Santa Claus--Juvenile poetry. 2. Christmas--Juvenile poetry. 3. Children's poetry, American. I. Wager-Smith, Curtis II. Title. III. Series: Classic reprint series (Almonte, Ont.)

PS2429.M5N5 2005   j811'.2   C2005-905330-5

Printed in Canada
#1-9-05

The History of
The Night Before Christmas

When Clement Clarke Moore first wrote this poem in 1822, he called it "A Visit from St. Nicholas". Legend has it that he composed the poem on Christmas Eve during a sleigh ride from Greenwich Village to his home. Further legend suggests that he described St. Nicholas in the image of the portly, bearded Dutchman who had driven him to the village and back that afternoon to buy the holiday turkey. Once he had read it to his wife and six children on that Christmas Eve in 1822 he apparently thought so little of the poem that he never bothered copyrighting it. A family friend submitted the poem to an upstate New York newspaper, The Sentinel, which published it anonymously the following Christmas. The poem was immediately popular, spreading across the country and shortly across the world. Only in 1844 did Moore include it in a book of his poetry.

Interestingly, Moore's father, the Reverend Benjamin Moore, was president of what later became Columbia University as well as being the Episcopal Bishop of New York. Reverend Moore was famous for giving the last rites to Alexander Hamilton after he was wounded in his 1804 duel with Aaron Burr. Clement Moore, born in 1779 to this distinguished family, was a well-known Hebrew scholar, and a real estate buyer and developer in Manhattan as well as speaking five languages and being an author. These achievements have faded away but he remains famous as the author of what he once called his "mere trifle", *The Night Before Christmas*.

Leonard G. Lee, Publisher
Almonte, Ontario
September 2005

In all the illustrations in this book you will be asked to find a hidden picture.
The answers to the puzzle pictures are at the back of this book.

THE

NIGHT BEFORE CHRISTMAS

ILLUSTRATED WITH PUZZLE PICTURES

By

CURTIS WAGER-SMITH

Algrove Publishing~Classic Reprint Series

Find the children's father

'TWAS the night before Christmas,
When all through the house
Not a creature was stirring,
Not even a mouse;

THE stockings were hung
            By the chimney with care,
In hopes that St. Nicholas
            Soon would be there;

Find the baby

THE children were nestled
                All snug in their beds,
While visions of sugar-plums
                Danced in their heads;

Find the doll that Mary is dreaming of

AND Mamma in her kerchief
                    And I in my cap,
Had just settled our brains
                    For a long winter's nap---

Find the mother

WHEN out on the lawn
      There rose such a clatter,
I sprang from my bed
      To see what was the matter;

Find the cat

AWAY to the window
               I flew like a flash,
Tore open the shutters
               And threw up the sash.

Find Johnny

THE moon, on the breast
　　　　Of the new-fallen snow,
Gave a luster of mid-day
　　　　To objects below:

Find Jack Frost

15

WHEN, what to my wondering eyes
                    Should appear,
But a miniature sleigh,
                    And eight tiny Reindeer:

Find an angel

WITH a little old driver,
So lively and quick,
I knew in a moment
It must be St. Nick;

Find St. Nick's dog

MORE rapid than eagles
                His coursers they came,
And he whistled, and shouted,
                And called them by name—

Find St. Nick

"NOW, Dasher! now, Dancer!
       Now, Prancer and Vixen!
On! Comet, on! Cupid,
       On! Dunder and Blitzen;

Find father carrying home a Christmas tree

TO the top of the porch,
To the top of the wall!
Now, dash away, dash away,
Dash away all!"

Find the trumpet that fell out of the sleigh

AS dry leaves that before
               The wild hurricane fly,
When they meet with an obstacle,
               Mount to the sky;

Find a snowbird

SO, up to the house-top
             The coursers they flew,
With sleigh full of toys---
             And Saint Nicholas too.

Find Johnny's hobby-horse

AND then in a twinkling
                    I heard on the roof
The prancing and pawing
                    Of each little hoof;

Find St. Nick's stable man

AS I drew in my head,
And was turning around,
Down the chimney St. Nicholas
Came with a bound.

Find a teddy bear

HE was dressed all in fur
    From his head to his foot
And his clothes were all tarnished
    With ashes and soot:

Find Johnny's fishing rod

A BUNDLE of toys
He had flung on his back,
And he looked like a peddler
Just opening his pack;

Find Prancer who followed St. Nick down the chimney

HIS eyes how they twinkled!
His dimples how merry!
His cheeks were like roses,
His nose like a cherry;

Find the boy

HIS droll little mouth
      Was drawn up like a bow,
And the beard on his chin
      Was as white as the snow!

Find a roller skate

THE stump of a pipe
          He held tight in his teeth,
And the smoke, it encircled
          His head like a wreath.

Find St. Nick's pipe

HE had a broad face,
    And a little round belly,
That shook when he laughed,
    Like a bowl-full of jelly.

Find St. Nick's little boy

HE was chubby and plump,
A right jolly old elf;
And I laughed when I saw him
In spite of myself.

Find St. Nick's wife

A WINK of his eye,
          And a twist of his head,
Soon gave me to know
          I had nothing to dread.

Find a jumping jack

HE spoke not a word,
But went straight to his work,
And filled all the stockings,
Then turned with a jerk,

Find Mary's pet lamb

AND laying his finger
　　　　　　　Aside of his nose,
And giving a nod,
　　　　　Up the chimney he rose.

Find a policeman

HE sprang to his sleigh,
         To his team gave a whistle,
And away they all flew,
         Like the down of a thistle:

Find the children's teacher

BUT I heard him exclaim
           Ere he drove out of sight,
  "Merry Christmas to all,
         And to all a Good Night."

THE END

Find the Christmas turkey

Answers to The Night Before Christmas Puzzle Pictures

LOCATIONS OF HIDDEN OBJECTS

ANSWERS TO PUZZLE PICTURES